How to Draw the Life and Times of
Ronald Reagan

Melody S. Mis

The Rosen Publishing Group's
PowerKids Press™
New York

To my helpers, Brian and Scott, who always make me laugh

Published in 2007 by The Rosen Publishing Group, Inc.
29 East 21st Street, New York, NY 10010

First Edition

Editor: Jennifer Way
Layout Design: Ginny Chu
Photo Researcher: Jeffrey Wendt

Illustrations: p. 27 by Ginny Chu, all other illustrations by Albert Hanner.
Photo Credits: pp. 4, 9, 10 AP/Wide World Photos; p. 7 Courtesy Ronald Reagan Library; p. 8 (left) Garren Zuck/presidentialavenue.com; p. 12 The "torch" logo is a registered trademark of Screen Actors Guild, Inc., and used with permission; p. 14 © Douglas Kirkland/Corbis; p. 16 © Bettmann/Corbis; p. 18 © 2001 One Mile Up, Inc.; p. 20 © Karl Weatherly/Corbis; p. 22 (left) Franz Jantzen, Collection of the Supreme Court of the United States; p.22 (right) Time Life Pictures/Getty Images; p. 24 NASA; p. 26 Library of Congress Geography and Map Division; p. 28 White House Historical Association (The White House Collection) (48).

Library of Congress Cataloging-in-Publication Data

Mis, Melody S.
How to draw the life and times of Ronald Reagan / Melody S. Mis.— 1st ed.
p. cm. — (A kid's guide to drawing the presidents of the United States of America) Includes index.
ISBN 1-4042-3016-5 (library binding)
1. Reagan, Ronald—Juvenile literature. 2. Presidents—United States—Biography—Juvenile literature.
3. Drawing—Technique—Juvenile literature. I. Title. II. Series.
E877.M57 2006
973.927'092—dc22

2005019742

Printed in China

Contents

Ronald Wilson Reagan

Ronald Wilson Reagan was born on February 6, 1911, in Tampico, Illinois, to John Edward and Nelle Wilson Reagan. When Reagan was nine years old, his family moved to Dixon, Illinois. In 1928, Reagan entered Eureka College in Eureka, Illinois, where he worked several jobs to pay for his education. After graduation from college in 1932, Reagan became a sports announcer for one of the nation's largest radio stations. It was located in Des Moines, Iowa.

In 1937, Reagan went to Los Angeles, California, to report on the Chicago Cubs baseball team. While he was in Los Angeles, he was discovered by Warner Brothers. The company hired him to act in movies. After the United States entered World War II in 1941, Reagan was called up by the army to make training films for the military.

From 1954 to 1962, Reagan hosted General Electric's *G.E. Theater*, a popular TV program. During his last years with General Electric, Reagan's political beliefs became increasingly conservative. His growing interest in politics and his popularity led him to run for governor of California.

In 1966, Reagan became California's Republican candidate for governor. He won the election easily and was reelected in 1970. The Republican Party nominated him as their presidential candidate in the 1980 election. He beat the Democratic candidate, President Jimmy Carter, and became the nation's fortieth president.

You will need the following supplies to draw the life and times of Ronald Reagan:

✓ A sketch pad   ✓ An eraser   ✓ A pencil   ✓ A ruler

These are some of the shapes and drawing terms you need to know:

Horizontal Line	——	Squiggly Line	
Oval		Trapezoid	
Rectangle		Triangle	
Shading		Vertical Line	
Slanted Line		Wavy Line	

The Great Communicator

Ronald Reagan was sworn in as president on January 20, 1981. At age 69, he was the oldest person to be elected president. He became known as the Great Communicator, because he had an easy manner of speaking to people.

Two months after Reagan took office, a man shot him in the chest. Reagan recovered and began to fulfill his campaign promises of reducing the national debt and cutting taxes. Reagan's presidency was hurt by a scandal, however. In 1985, the United States sold weapons to Iran in exchange for their help in getting American hostages in Lebanon freed. Lebanon is in the Middle East. Government officials then took money made from the weapons' sale and sent it to people in Central America who were trying to overthrow their government. These events became known as the Iran-Contra scandal. The scandal stained Reagan's presidency but did not have a lasting effect on his popularity.

Reagan was known as the Great Communicator in part because he was good at convincing people to accept his ideas. As president he made many speeches. Here Reagan is shown making a speech in 1981.

Reagan in Illinois

This is Reagan's birthplace in Tampico, Illinois.

Illinois

Map of the United States of America

Ronald Reagan was born in Tampico, Illinois, on February 6, 1911. His birthplace has been rebuilt to look the way it did when the family lived there. The home is a museum that is open to the public. Tampico became part of the Reagan Trail, which was created by the state of Illinois to honor him. The trail connects all the places that were part of Reagan's life in Illinois.

Eureka, Illinois, is also part of the Reagan Trail, because Reagan attended college there from 1928 to 1932. Reagan visited Eureka College several times after he graduated. Eureka College honored Reagan by putting a sculpture of him at the place where he gave a speech. The school also named a garden, called the Reagan Peace Garden, after him. The garden features a piece of the Berlin Wall, which was torn down in 1989, to celebrate the end of the cold war. The wall had separated Communist East Germany from democratic West Germany. During a speech in 1987, Reagan told the Soviet leader Mikhail Gorbachev to

This statue of Reagan stands near his childhood home in Dixon, Illinois.

"tear down this wall!" A year and a half later, the wall was torn down, and pieces of it ended up as souvenirs.

Reagan's Boyhood Home

In 1920, the Reagans moved to nearby Dixon, Illinois. Ronald Reagan and his older brother, Neil, used to play football with friends. They also liked to fish and swim in the Rock River, which ran through the town. When Reagan was 15, he was hired as a lifeguard at Lowell Park, which was located on the Rock River. He held this job for seven summers, during which he saved 77 people from drowning.

In high school Reagan was outgoing and popular with the other students. He played football and basketball and joined the drama club. It was from his drama teacher that Reagan learned basic acting skills.

In 1980, a group in Dixon raised enough money to purchase Reagan's boyhood home, which had been put up for sale. They fixed up the home, shown here, so that it would look the way it did in 1920.

1 To begin drawing Reagan's childhood home, make a rectangular guide. Add two slanted rectangles. This will be your guide for the front porch.

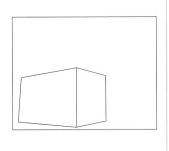

2 Draw seven slanted rectangles as shown. Notice that they are all different sizes. These will be your guides for drawing the other parts of the house.

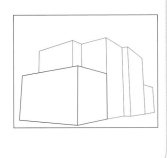

3 Add roofs to the house by making triangular and trapezoidal shapes. Make the edges of the roofs by drawing straight lines.

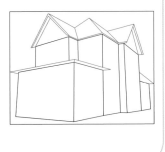

4 Add windows to the house by making six rectangles. Draw the small window on the front of the house by making a diamond shape. Begin drawing the porch by drawing three rectangles and two smaller shapes as shown.

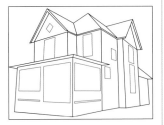

5 Draw the front porch using rectangles and straight lines. Notice where the railings and the doors will go. Add the porch's steps as shown.

6 Draw the chimney using rectangles. Add detail to the porch windows and the windows on the side of the house. Draw the back porch and the details on the side of the house. Add handrails beside the steps.

7 Add detail to the windows on the upper floor of the house using rectangles and straight lines. Erase the rectangular guide you drew in step 1.

8 Add shading and detail. Notice that it is darker under the porch and beneath the roofs. Great job!

Reagan Goes to Hollywood

After Ronald Reagan graduated from college, he worked as a radio sports announcer. In 1937, he moved to Hollywood, California, to work for Warner Brothers.

In 1938, Reagan met the actress Jane Wyman, whom he married in 1940. The couple had two children before they divorced in 1948. In 1941, Reagan was ordered into service by the army to make training films for World War II fighter pilots. He did this until the war ended in 1945.

In 1941, Reagan joined the board of the Screen Actors Guild (SAG), which is the actors' union. He served as its president for six years. The SAG logo is shown above. As president of the guild, he helped improve working conditions and get better salaries for its members. It was while Reagan was president of the guild that he met Nancy Davis, whom he married in 1952.

1

Begin drawing the SAG logo by making a rectangular guide.

2

Draw two curved shapes. They will be your guide for drawing the ranches. Make a guide for the torch by drawing an oval shape and a curved shape underneath it.

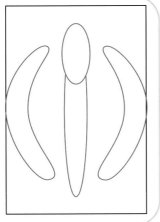

3

Draw the outline of the torch using curved shapes and straight lines. Add a circle to the bottom of the torch.

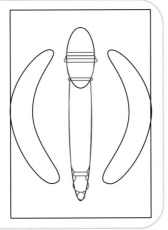

4

Add the flames at the top of the torch by making zigzag and curved lines.

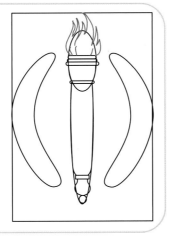

5

Erase the torch guidelines you drew in step 2. Outline the letters S, A, G.

6

Add the ribbons to the bottom part of the logo using curved lines. Erase the lines that go through the letters you drew in step 5.

7

Draw leaves inside the guidelines you drew in step 2. Notice that the leaves are egg shaped and that most of them have a line in the middle of them.

8

Erase the guidelines for the branches you drew in step 2. Add shading and detail. Wonderful work!

Meet Nancy Reagan

Nancy Davis was born on July 6, 1921, in New York City, to Edith and Kenneth Robbins. Shortly after Nancy's birth, her parents divorced. In 1929, her mother married Loyal Davis. After Nancy graduated from high school, she attended Smith College in Northampton, Massachusetts, where she studied acting. She graduated in 1943, and became an actress. Nancy met Ronald Reagan in Hollywood in 1949. They married in 1952, and had two children. She supported Reagan in his movie career and in his political life.

As First Lady Nancy supported the Foster Grandparent Program, which encouraged older people to help orphaned or disabled children. She also led the "Just Say No" campaign, which taught children about how harmful drugs can be. Nancy and President Reagan helped talented young people by inviting them to perform at the White House. Today Nancy lives at the Reagan ranch near Santa Barbara, California.

1

Begin your picture of Nancy Reagan by making a rectangular guide.

2

Draw the outline of her body using straight lines. Draw a guide for her head by making an oval. Draw the outline of her hair as shown.

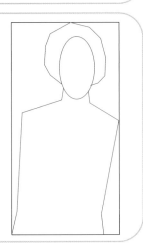

3

Draw two crossing lines on the head to make a guide for drawing the face. Add guides for her forehead, eyes, nose, and mouth. Add her hair using squiggly lines. Make the neckline of her dress using a curved line.

4

Draw the details of her face and neck by making curved lines. Add more hair using wavy lines. Add her earrings using curved lines and circular shapes as shown.

5

Using the guide you drew in step 2, draw the outline of her clothes. Add the collar to her jacket by drawing curved lines. Draw the bow of her blouse.

6

Finish drawing her jacket using curved lines. Add folds to the jacket using squiggly lines. Draw pockets on the jacket by making curved and straight lines.

7

Erase the face guides you drew in step 3. Erase the body, hair, and head guidelines you drew in step 2. Draw three buttons on her jacket and a button on each pocket using circles and curved lines.

8

Finish your drawing by adding shading and detail. Well done!

Switching Parties

In 1962, Ronald Reagan made a decision that would change his life. He left the Democratic Party to become a Republican. The elephant shown here is the symbol of the Republican Party.

As a young man, Reagan had been a Democrat. His political beliefs changed, however, after he began working for General Electric and visiting with its workers in the 1950s. He realized that workers, who struggled to provide for their own families, were forced to pay taxes to support the government's programs that helped people in need. This led him to join the more conservative Republican Party in 1962. Reagan agreed with the Republican idea of a small government and low taxes. Reagan became a rising star in the Republican Party when he gave a campaign speech for the 1964 Republican presidential candidate Barry Goldwater. Reagan's growing popularity caught the attention of the California Republican Party, which asked him to run for governor in 1966.

1

You will be drawing the Republican Party elephant. To begin make a square guide.

2

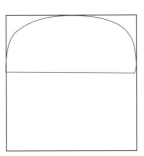

Draw a line across the guide square. Add a curved line at the top of the guide square. This will be the elephant's back.

3

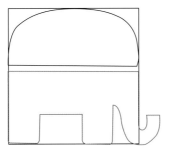

Draw a line across the guide square. Add the elephant's legs by making seven straight lines. Make the elephant's trunk using curved and straight lines.

4

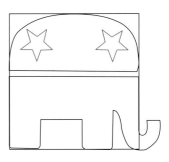

Draw stars on either side of the top half of the elephant.

5

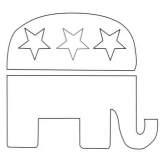

Erase the square guide you drew in step 1. Draw a star between the two stars you drew in step 4.

6

Add shading. Notice that the top of the elephant is darker than the bottom and that the stars are not shaded. Good job!

Governor of California

During the campaign for governor, Ronald Reagan ran against the state's Democratic governor Pat Brown. Brown made fun of Reagan, because he was an actor and had just made a movie called *Bedtime for Bonzo*, which starred a chimpanzee.

Reagan went on to beat Governor Brown by one million votes. The Great Seal of California, shown here, decorates the capitol in Sacramento. After Reagan took office on January 3, 1967, he decreased the state's debt by cutting government spending. Reagan was so popular with Californians that they elected him to a second term in 1970. In 1971, Reagan signed the California Welfare Reform Act, which took many people off welfare and increased the aid to those who were most in need. Reagan's success as governor put him in the national spotlight and caused Republicans to nominate him for president in the 1980 election.

1 Begin drawing the California seal by making two guide circles. Notice that the smaller circle is inside the bigger circle.

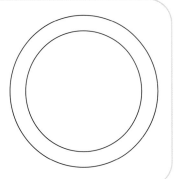

2 Draw a circle inside the larger circle you drew in step 1. Write the words "THE GREAT SEAL OF THE STATE OF" and "CALIFORNIA" between this circle and the smaller circle.

3 Inside the smaller circle, draw the outline of Minerva. Minerva is the Roman goddess of wisdom. Add the spear and the shield Minerva holds. Next to Minerva draw the outline of the bear as shown.

4 Draw the details of Minerva's helmet and clothes. Add details to the shield as shown. Begin to draw the background using squiggly lines.

5 Add mountains to the background using squiggly lines. Draw the land in the foreground using curved lines.

6 Draw the five ships in the water in the background as shown. In the sky above the spear, write the word "EUREKA." This word is the state's motto. It is Greek for "I have found it."

7 Draw the gold miner and his tools in the background as shown. Gold was discovered in California in 1849, which drew people to settle there. Add the grain near the bear in the foreground.

8 Add shading and detail to the seal. You did a great job on this drawing!

The 1980 Olympics

After Ronald Reagan left the governor's office in 1975, he campaigned to become the 1976 Republican presidential candidate, but the Republicans nominated President Gerald Ford instead. Ford lost the presidential election to the Democrat Jimmy Carter.

During Carter's last year in office, the 1980 Olympics were to be held in Moscow, in the Soviet Union. The Olympics are represented by the flag shown here. The United States and 50 other countries decided not to take part in the Olympics to protest the Soviet Union's attack on Afghanistan. In 1979, the Soviets had begun fighting to take control of Afghanistan, which is in Asia.

When Reagan became the Republican candidate in the 1980 presidential election, he worried that the Soviet Union might attack the United States. Reagan campaigned on the promise to make the military stronger. On election day Reagan received eight million more votes than Carter and won the presidency.

1

You will be drawing the Olympic flag. Start by making a square guide.

2

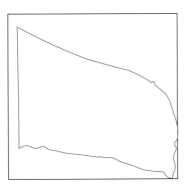

Inside the guide draw the outline of the flag using straight, curved, and squiggly lines.

3

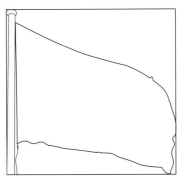

Draw the flagpole. Add the shape to the top of the pole and the string as shown.

4

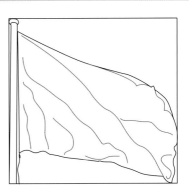

Draw the folds on the flag using squiggly lines.

5

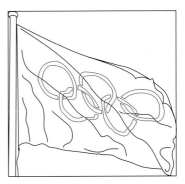

Draw the five rings on the flag. These rings stand for the five parts of the world that join in the Olympics. These are the Americas, Australia, Africa, Asia, and Europe.

6

Color your flag using the picture as a guide. The rings are blue, black, red, yellow, and green. Good job!

The First Woman
Supreme Court Justice

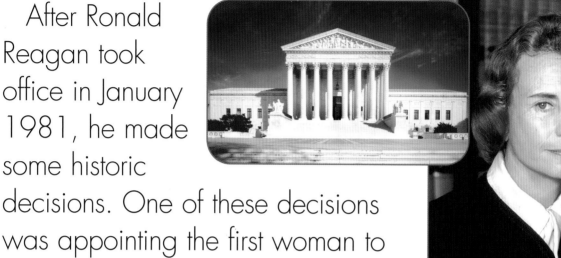

After Ronald Reagan took office in January 1981, he made some historic decisions. One of these decisions was appointing the first woman to serve on the Supreme Court, which is the highest court in the country. During his campaign he had promised to choose a woman for this position. In 1981, he nominated Sandra Day O'Connor.

O'Connor served in the Supreme Court building, shown here, which is in Washington, D.C. Supreme Court judges are appointed by the president and serve until they either quit or die. In 1979, O'Connor had been appointed to the Arizona Court of Appeals, which was one of the highest courts in the state. Her conservative decisions as a part of that court caught Reagan's attention, so he appointed her to the Supreme Court. In July 2005, O'Connor announced that she would step down from the Supreme Court once a new justice was appointed.

1

You will be drawing the Supreme Court building in Washington, D.C. To begin make a rectangular guide.

2

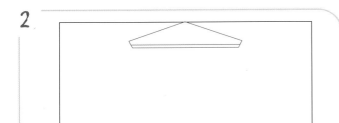

Inside the rectangular guide, draw the roof using a triangle. Add a long, thin rectangle under the triangle.

3

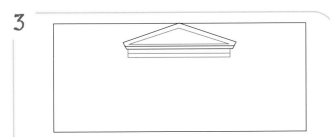

Draw a triangle inside the one you drew in step 2. Add two more long, thin rectangles. This triangular part of the building is called the pediment.

4

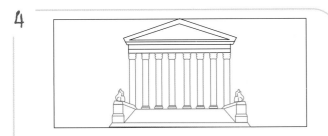

Under the pediment draw eight columns using straight lines and curved lines. Add a trapezoid where the steps will be. On either side of the steps, draw the statues as shown.

5

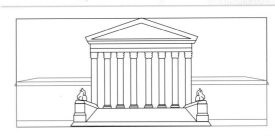

Draw the sides of the Supreme Court building using straight lines and slanted lines.

6

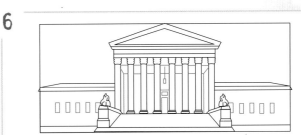

Add 10 windows to the sides of the building using rectangles. Draw the door to the building using rectangles. Add the details to the space between the door and the columns as shown.

7

Draw the steps to the front of the building by making many straight horizontal lines. Add bushes to the sides of the building using squiggly lines.

8

Add shading and detail. Notice that the windows and the steps are the darkest. Wonderful job!

The *Challenger*

In the 1984 presidential election, Ronald Reagan beat the Democratic candidate, Walter Mondale, by winning 59 percent of the popular vote. During his second term in office, a terrible event happened. On January 28, 1986, the *Challenger* space shuttle exploded, killing all seven crew members. Millions of people watched the launch on television, because a teacher was traveling on board the space shuttle. Christa McAuliffe taught social studies at a high school in Concord, New Hampshire. She and the other crew members drew the plans for the patch shown here.

Reagan appointed a group to find out what caused the *Challenger* disaster. It took four months to discover that a flawed part of the shuttle had caused it to explode. The government stopped the space program for almost three years. In 1988, the space program began again with the successful launch of the shuttle *Discovery*.

1 You will be drawing the patch that the *Challenger* crew wore. To begin draw two circles. Notice that the smaller circle is inside the larger circle.

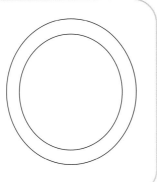

2 Draw a circle on the left side of the patch. Inside the circles you drew in step 1, add curved lines that follow the circles. Make sure that these lines do not go through the circle on the left.

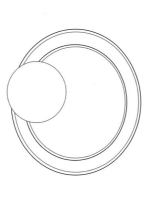

3 On the right side of the patch, draw the *Challenger* space shuttle as shown. Make sure to erase any lines that go through the space shuttle.

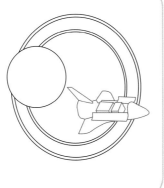

4 Draw the shape at the bottom of the patch using curved lines. Add a curved line to the circle you drew in step 2. Draw the curved lines behind the *Challenger* and add details to it.

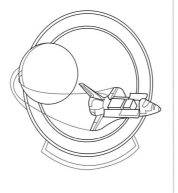

5 Erase the lines that go through the lines behind the *Challenger* that you drew in step 4. Add the shape on the right as shown. Draw the globe in the left circle.

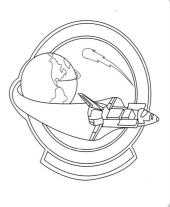

6 Write the names "MCNAIR," "ONIZUKA," "RESNIK," "SCOBEE," "SMITH," "MCAULIFFE," and "JARVIS" in the patch as shown. These are the names of the astronauts.

7 Draw the stars and stripes of the American flag in the background as shown. Notice that some of the stars and stripes are covered by other things in the patch.

8 Shade your drawing. You did a great job!

25

The End of the Cold War

Ronald Reagan is praised as the president who brought an end to the cold war between the United States and the Soviet Union, shown here.
The cold war began after the end of World War II, in 1945. During the cold war, the two countries did not fight. Instead they competed to see who could create the most deadly weapons. Reagan wanted the two countries to find a way to make peace. This was hard in the beginning of Reagan's presidency, because the Soviet leaders were not interested in working with American leaders for peace.

This changed in 1985, when Mikhail Gorbachev became the Soviet Union's leader. Gorbachev wanted to have a better relationship with the United States and end the weapons race. In 1987, he and Reagan signed a treaty, which called for both countries to get rid of some weapons. This treaty led to later treaties that ended the cold war.

1

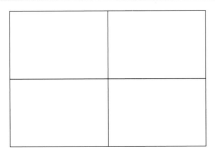

To begin drawing a map of the Soviet Union, make a rectangular guide. Draw a horizontal and vertical line in the center.

2

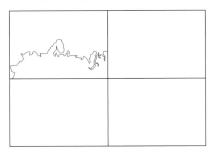

Starting at the top left corner, draw the northwest border using squiggly lines.

3

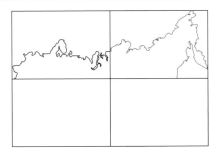

Continue drawing the northeast border using squiggly lines.

4

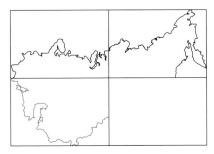

Now draw the southwest border using squiggly lines.

5

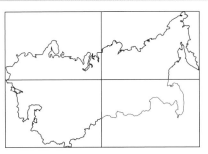

Finish the southwest border on the bottom right corner of the box as shown.

6

Erase the rectangular guide and the guidelines. Draw the islands around the northern and eastern borders. In the center write "SOVIET UNION."

7

Using squiggly lines draw the rivers and lakes that run through the country.

8

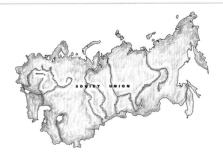

Finish the drawing by shading and adding in details. Well done!

Reagan's Legacy

Ronald Reagan left office on January 20, 1989, and retired to his ranch near Santa Barbara, California. Reagan remained in good health until 1994, when he was told that he had Alzheimer's, which is an illness of the brain that affects a person's memory. He died at age 93 on June 5, 2004.

Reagan was the most popular president since Franklin D. Roosevelt. Some people called Reagan the Grandfather of the Nation, because he was the oldest man to serve as president. During his presidency Reagan created millions of jobs, decreased government spending, cut taxes, strengthened the military, and helped end the cold war. Even though the Iran-Contra scandal took place during Reagan's presidency, it did not affect his popularity in the long run. Some historians rank Reagan as one of the top U.S. presidents.

1

To begin your picture of Ronald Reagan, draw a rectangular guide.

2

Inside the guide, draw the outline of his body using straight and slanted lines. Add an oval as a guide for his head. Draw two lines that cross inside the head guide. This will help you draw his face.

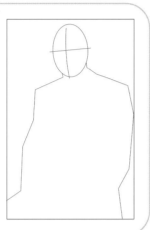

3

Draw the outline of his clothes using straight lines. Add the outline of his hand. Draw the outline of his hair. Add guides for Reagan's eyes, nose, mouth, and neck.

4

Draw Reagan's face using the guidelines you drew in step 2 and the guides you drew in step 3. Draw his ear using curved and squiggly lines. Finish his hair using wavy lines.

5

Draw Reagan's jacket, tie, and shirt using straight, curved, and slanted lines as shown. Add the details to his hands as shown.

6

Erase the rectangular guide and the head guide. Draw the collar of the jacket using slanted lines. Add the folds of the jacket and the handkerchief using squiggly lines. Draw his cufflink and his watch.

7

Add shading and detail. You did a wonderful job!

Timeline

1911   Ronald Reagan is born on February 6, in Tampico, Illinois.

1920   The Reagans move to Dixon, Illinois.

1928-1932   Reagan attends Eureka College in Eureka, Illinois.

1937   Warner Brothers hires Reagan.

1940   Reagan marries Jane Wyman.

1941   Reagan joins the Screen Actors Guild.
The army drafts Reagan to make training films during World War II.

1948   Reagan and Wyman divorce.

1952   Reagan marries Nancy Davis.

1962   Reagan joins the Republican Party.

1967-1975   Reagan serves as governor of California.

1981-1989   Reagan serves as president of the United States.

1987   Reagan and Gorbachev sign the INF Treaty, which reduced weapons.

1989   Reagan retires to his California ranch.

2004   Reagan dies at home in California on June 5.

Glossary

cold war (KOLD WOR) A struggle between the Soviet Union and the United States and western Europe that lasted from the end of World War II in 1945 until 1990. It was marked by the race between the Soviets and Americans to create deadly weapons.

communicator (kuh-MYOO-nih-kayt-er) One who easily shares facts or feelings.

Communist (KOM-yuh-nist) Belonging to a system in which all the land, houses, and factories belong to the government and are shared by everyone.

conservative (kun-SER-vuh-tiv) Favoring a course of keeping things as they are.

debt (DET) Something owed.

disaster (dih-ZAS-ter) An event that causes suffering or loss.

drama (DRAH-muh) Having to do with a play or a skit.

hostages (HOS-tij-ez) People who are held as prisoners until some condition is agreed to.

launch (LONCH) The sending off of a spacecraft into the air.

legacy (LEH-guh-see) Something left behind by a person's actions.

motto (MAH-toh) Words that stand for something or that state what someone believes.

nominated (NAH-muh-nayt-ed) Selected to do a certain job.

orphaned (OR-fund) Without parents.

ranch (RANCH) A large farm for raising cattle, horses, or sheep.

scandal (SKAN-dul) Conduct that people find shocking and bad.

shuttle (SHUH-tul) A type of spaceship.

souvenirs (SOO-veh-nirz) Things that are kept as a reminder of something, usually a trip.

symbol (SIM-bul) An object or a picture that stands for something else.

welfare (WEL-fer) The money that is given to poor people so they can improve their living conditions.

Index

Web Sites

Due to the changing nature of Internet links, PowerKids Press has developed an online list of Web sites related to the subject of this book. This site is updated regularly. Please use this link to access the list:
www.powerkidslinks.com/kgdpusa/reagan/